FUN WITH

SCIENCE

By Mae and Ira Freeman

SCHOLASTIC INC.

NEW YORK · TORONTO · LONDON · AUCKLAND · SYDNEY · TOKYO

Other books by
Mae and Ira Freeman
available through
Scholastic Book Services:

FUN WITH ASTRONOMY
FUN WITH CHEMISTRY

ISBN 0-590-36008-6

CONTENTS

Scientists do experiments to find out exactly what happens in our surroundings. Then they try to put the results together to make scientific laws.

The experiments in this book will help you understand some of the important laws of science. Be sure to do all the experiments, so that you can see for yourself how scientific laws work.

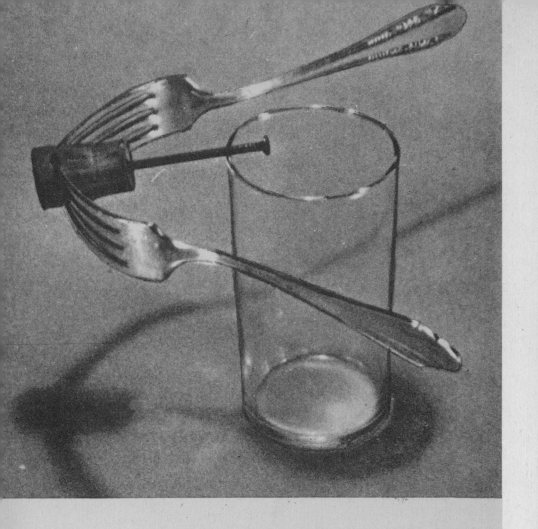

Stick a nail and two forks into a cork, as in the picture. Rest the nail on the rim of a drinking glass and slide the nail slowly across the rim until you can make the forks balance. You have now found the center of gravity of the balanced forks. It is just where the nail rests on the edge of the glass.

THINGS STANDING STILL

Many of the things in the world around us are at rest and stay where they are put. The weight of a chair makes it press down on the floor. At the same time, the floor must be pushing upward on the chair just as hard, otherwise the chair would fall. Things at rest remain still because all the pushes and pulls they get from their surroundings are in balance.

Begin your experimenting by finding out what must be done to make things stay in place.

First, lay a pencil flat on the table, and it stays just where you put it. But if you try to stand the pencil on its point, it falls over every time. How can a tightrope walker keep from falling? Is there any danger that the Empire State Building could topple over?

There is a certain point in every object where the whole weight seems to center. This point is called the **center of gravity.** Once you find this point, you can balance the object there.

The center of gravity of a straight stick is right at its middle. A twelve-inch ruler can be balanced by putting your finger under it at the six-inch mark.

The center of gravity of a thing is not always where you think it is, and sometimes you may be fooled by what you see.

Get a round box with a flat rim, so that it can roll like a wheel. A cardboard cheese box is good for this experiment. Tape a marble to the inside of the rim, as in the picture. Before closing the box, make a small mark on the outside so you will know exactly where the marble is.

Place one book on another to make a slope, as the picture shows. Now hold the box near the top of the slope, with the hidden weight just a little on the *downhill* side of the box. When you let go, the box rolls down the hill as you expect.

Next, set the box near the bottom of the hill, with the hidden weight a little on the *uphill* side. This time the box rolls *up* the hill!

This is what happened: The center of gravity of the box is not at the middle, where everybody expects it to be. Instead, it is near the edge, where you attached the marble. In both of the tests, the center of gravity went down as the box rolled. But in the second test, the whole box had to roll uphill so that the hidden weight could go down. Your experiment showed that the center of gravity always moves to get as low as possible.

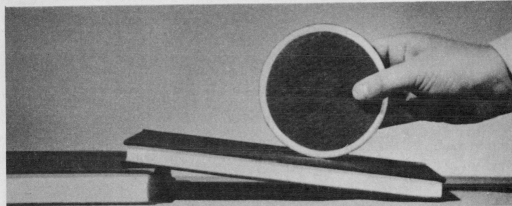

If you know how to set the box on the slope . . .

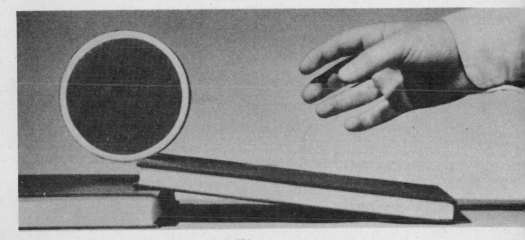

. . . it will roll uphill!

You know that things cannot start moving all by themselves. And you know, too, how hard it is to start a heavy object moving. Scientists have a name for this kind of "laziness" of things. They call it **inertia**.

Suppose you are sitting in a car and the driver starts it suddenly. You fall back in your seat because the inertia of your body makes it try to stay where it is.

It is also true that if a thing is already moving, it will keep moving until something stops it. If you are riding in a car and the brakes are put on suddenly, you pitch forward because your body tends to keep going.

Test these ideas by an experiment. Place a card on top of a drinking glass, and lay a quarter on the card. Send the card flying with a sharp snap of your finger, making sure not to tip the card upward as you strike it. The quarter stays behind and falls into the glass. The inertia of the coin keeps it from going along with the card.

When the card is snapped out . . .

. . . the coin stays back.

Hang a heavy book from a doorknob with a piece of string. Tie a piece of the same string to the bottom of the book, as in the picture. Pull down evenly and steadily on the lower string. The top string will break, because it was being pulled by your hand and by the weight of the book too.

Now try the experiment again. This time hold the lower string slack and then give it a quick downward jerk. It will break, but the upper string will not.

The heavy book has great inertia. It cannot start fast enough to break the upper string before the lower string snaps.

Which string will break?

10

THINGS IN MOTION

Cars whiz by on the road, birds skim through the air, elevators carry people from floor to floor in tall buildings, the earth spins. All these things are moving, and the motion follows scientific laws.

The great scientist Isaac Newton watched and studied things in motion. Then he was able to form scientific laws that tell about motion of every kind.

You know that a locomotive has to pull very hard to get a train started. You also know that the train will keep moving for a long distance after the power is shut off, unless the engineer uses the brakes. Newton realized that every moving thing keeps right on moving unless something acts to stop it.

A weight swinging around in a circle keeps pulling outward from the center. Why? What makes a rocket zoom through the air? Why does a gun kick? You can find the answers to these questions by doing the experiments on the next few pages.

When you ride in a car going around a sharp curve, you feel as though you are being pressed toward the outside of the curve. This is because your body tends to keep going straight ahead, but the turning of the car does not let it. Anything that moves swiftly around a curve pulls toward the outside.

Put a piece of heavy string through the hole in a large spool. Tie one end of the string to a smaller spool and the other end to a potato.

Hold the larger spool in your hand and start the smaller spool swinging around and around in a level circle overhead, as in the picture. When the small spool is going fast enough, its outward-moving force will lift the much heavier potato.

In ancient times, long before gunpowder was invented, the catapult was an important weapon of war. It was used to send a heavy stone through the air with great speed.

To make a catapult, place a ruler on a table with a shorter part over the edge, as in the picture. Lay a rubber eraser on the other end. Now give the short end a sharp downward blow with your fist. The eraser flies upward much faster than your hand comes down. Can you tell why? You can if you remember that the part of the ruler on the table is longer than the part over the edge.

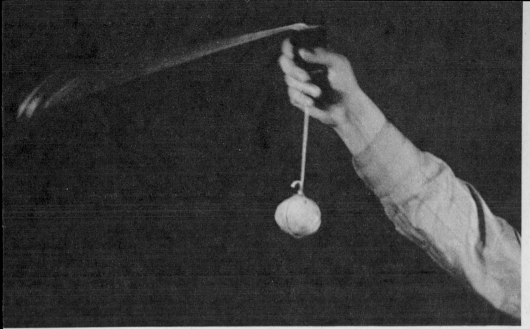

The whirling spool lifts the heavy potato.

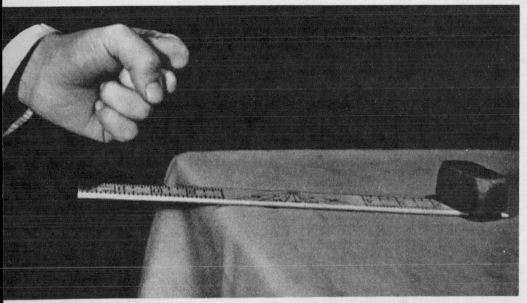

Hit the ruler with your fist and send the eraser flying.

In baseball, bowling, tennis, and other games, the movements of the ball can be explained by scientific laws.

In bowling, there is a rack where the returned balls line up. Whenever another ball comes along and hits the row, the ball at the far end jumps away if there is room. All the others remain perfectly still. The bump is passed on through all the balls, but only the last one is free to be knocked away.

Test this law of motion. Instead of the bowling-ball rack, use a groove formed by taping two rulers side by side, as in the picture. For the balls, use marbles that are all the same size. Place several marbles in the groove, making sure that they touch each other. Then, with a snap of your finger, roll one marble toward the row. The end marble will spring away, while all the others stay right where they are. If you send two marbles toward the row, two jump off at the other end. It works this way with any number of marbles.

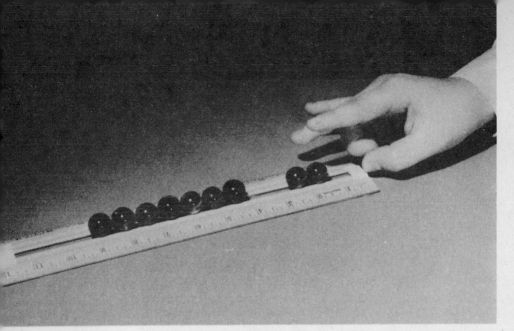

Send two marbles toward the row . . .

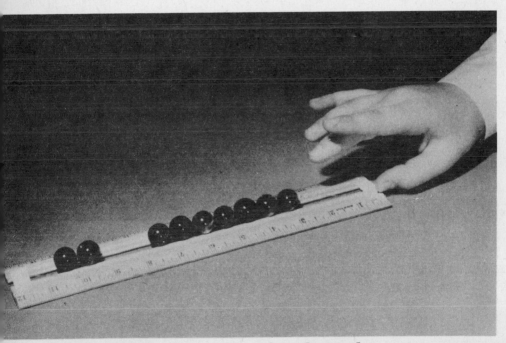

. . . and two jump off at the other end.

Pour in the vinegar and quickly cork the bottle.

Jet action sends the bottle backward.

Place a broom across the top of two chairs, and hang a bottle from the broomstick with two long strings. The bottle should hang level just a few inches off the floor.

Put about two tablespoons of baking soda into the bottle. Use a funnel to pour in about a quarter of a glass of vinegar. Then quickly cork the bottle — not too tightly — and let it hang by the cords. In a moment or two the cork will shoot out with a loud "pop," and the bottle will swing back, as in the lower picture.

The vinegar and baking soda form large amounts of carbon dioxide gas inside the bottle. The pressure of the gas makes the cork shoot forward and the bottle swing backward.

This experiment is an example of the scientific law of action and reaction. It shows that when anything starts moving, it must kick back on something else. You cannot have one without the other.

The law of action and reaction explains how rockets and jets fly. Gases shoot out of the rear, and the reaction drives the rocket itself forward. It does not need air around to help it move because it reacts on its own gases. That is why a rocket can travel in outer space.

When a stone falls, does it drop at a steady speed or does it fall faster and faster? Experiments prove that a falling weight gains speed from the moment it is let go.

Test this yourself. Get a ten-foot length of string and four potatoes. Tie a potato firmly to one end of the string. Tie another a foot farther along. Fasten the next three feet farther on, and the last one five feet beyond that.

Stand on a high place and hold the string so that the lowest potato just clears the ground. Then let go. You will hear equally spaced thumps, even though the potatoes are not at all equally spaced along the string.

You proved that a weight takes only *twice* as long to fall four feet as it takes to fall one foot. And it takes only *three* times as long to fall *nine* feet. This shows that a dropped weight keeps picking up speed at a steady rate as it falls.

18

Listen for the thumps as the potatoes fall.

A liquid presses on anything placed in it. It presses not only downward, but sideways and upward as well. You can feel the upward force if you push a block of wood down into a pail of water.

Because of this pressure, anything placed in a liquid seems lighter in weight. In one of the experiments you will find out why some things float in water and others do not.

Archimedes, a great Greek philosopher who lived more than two thousand years ago, discovered the law that tells about floating and sinking. Once when he was bathing in the public baths, he noticed that his body seemed to be lighter in weight when under water. He ran home at once to test the idea further, forgetting in his excitement to put on his clothes!

In many branches of science and engineering, it is important to understand the actions of liquids.

A submarine must have a strong hull to hold back the pressure of the sea. If a submarine goes too deep, it may be crushed like an eggshell.

The deeper the water, the harder it presses. The deepest spot in the ocean is about 36,000 feet down. At this depth, the water pushes with a force of nearly eight tons on every square inch!

How can a fish that lives deep in the sea stand these great pressures without being crushed? The answer is that the fish has the same amount of pressure inside its body, pushing outward. If one of these creatures is caught and hauled quickly to the surface, the inside pressure does not drop fast enough to equal the outside pressure, so the poor fish actually blows up!

Here is an interesting way to show that the deeper the water, the harder it pushes. Use a nail to punch several holes down the side of a tin can. Put the can under a stream of running water so that it stays full while jets of water shoot from the holes.

Notice that the jets coming from the lower holes reach out farther. This shows that the push of the water is greatest near the bottom.

The deeper the water, the harder it pushes out.

A stone weighs more than a piece of wood of the same size. A quart of water weighs more than a quart of oil. In scientific words, a stone is more **dense** than wood, and water is more dense than oil. An object can float in a liquid only if it is less dense than the liquid.

To prove this, place a fresh egg in a glass of water. If it is perfectly fresh, there will be no gas in it and the egg will rest on the bottom. Now dissolve about two tablespoons of salt in the water, and the egg will slowly rise and float. Adding salt makes the liquid more dense than the egg.

Stick a thumbtack into the eraser end of a pencil. This will make the pencil float straight up and down in a glass of water, as in the first picture. Make a mark on the side of the pencil where the water line comes.

Float the same pencil in a glass of strong salt water and notice that it now rides higher. This is because salt water is more dense than plain water.

In this experiment you made an instrument called a **hydrometer**. A hydrometer is a float that is marked to tell how dense a liquid is. This instrument is very important in the work of engineers and chemists. Service stations use one to test the antifreeze liquid in the radiator of a car.

Which glass has salt water in it?

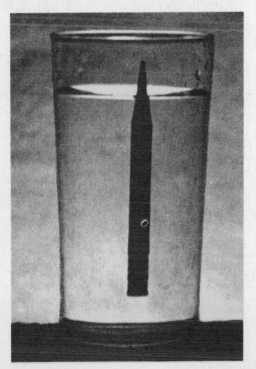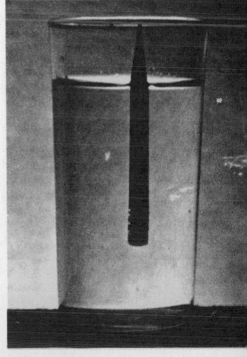

A homemade hydrometer.

Air pressing from the outside pushes the water up.

Stand a lighted candle firmly in the center of a soup plate, with a drop of melted wax. Pour water into the plate until it is almost full.

Now place a milk bottle over the candle, as in the picture. Soon you will see the water begin to rise inside the bottle. Then the candle flame goes out.

The flame went out when it used up some of the oxygen in the bottle. Because the remaining part of the air took up less room, the outside air was able to push water up into the bottle.

WATER'S INVISIBLE SKIN

If you watch drops falling from a faucet, or rain dripping from a window sill, you will notice that each drop hangs like a little rubber balloon full of water, until it breaks away. Every water surface seems to be covered with a tightly stretched skin. This is called **surface tension.**

The scientific explanation is that all the tiny molecules of water stick to one another very tightly. Because of this bunching together, the surface of a liquid becomes as small as possible. It acts as if it were made of stretched rubber.

Surface tension shows itself clearly in a soap bubble. The water of the bubble is stretched so thin that a hundred thousand layers would be only an inch thick. A big bubble on an open bubble pipe will get smaller and smaller as surface tension draws it together.

Surface tension is important in getting things clean. Most dirt that sticks to your clothes or your hands is held by a thin layer of oil or grease. Soap and detergents weaken the surface tension of the grease, so that the dirt can be rinsed away.

How is this possible? For the answer, look closely at the surface of the water. It curves up all around the edge of the blade. This means that the steel is resting *on top* of the water and is not floating *in* the water like a boat. Surface tension holds it up. Insects that skim over the surface of a pond are able to "walk on water" for the same reason.

When the great scientist Michael Faraday was a student, he carelessly left a towel hanging over the edge of a partly filled washbowl. When he awoke the next morning, he was surprised to find the bowl empty and the water in a pool on the floor. He figured out that surface tension had moved the water along in the tiny spaces between the threads of the towel. When the water reached the top of the bowl, its weight made it flow over the edge and onto the floor.

You can do Faraday's experiment. Place a handkerchief in a jar of water, letting one end hang over the side. Later, you will find that surface tension has lifted the water over the edge and let it drop into the glass.

**What keeps
the razor blade
from sinking?**

**Surface tension
lifts the water
through the
handkerchief.**

When soap dissolves in water, it weakens the surface tension. Even the smallest bit of soap is enough to change the surface tension of a large amount of water.

To show this, sprinkle pepper lightly and evenly over some water in a clean soup plate. The pepper has no effect on the water. It is used only to make the surface easy to see.

Now touch the water near one edge of the dish with a wet bar of soap. The moment the bar reaches it, the water on the surface snaps back to the opposite side of the dish, as you can see by the movement of the pepper.

THROUGH THE AIR

The only time we notice air is when it is in motion. Air can do surprising things when it is moving fast. It can uproot trees, lift the roofs off houses, and cause other destruction.

If you put your hand out of the window of a moving car, you can feel the backward push of the air. Actually, your hand is moving and the air is still, but the result is the same as when your hand is still and the air moves past it.

Leaves and pieces of paper do not crash to the ground like stones. They drift down slowly, held back by the air.

Engineers who design automobiles, airplanes, rockets, and large guns must have a good understanding of the resistance of the air to things that move through it. The resistance depends very much on the shape of the object. An object that has a **streamlined** shape will not churn up the air behind it when it moves.

Nature is an excellent streamline engineer. Birds and fishes have shapes that let them move at high speed through the air or water with very little effort.

As long as air is not moving, it presses equally in all directions. But when air moves past an object, it does not press as hard as air that is not moving. Find out what happens by doing an experiment.

Cut a strip of thick paper or light cardboard about two inches wide and one foot long. Tape the ends together and curve the paper little by little until the whole loop has the shape of the side view of an airplane wing, as in the picture.

Slip a pencil through the loop and hold it in the stream of air from an electric fan. The loop lifts up and stays level.

Now block off the air from the top of the wing with a stiff cardboard, as shown in the second picture. As the edge of the cardboard comes down, the end of the wing drops. This shows that some of the lifting was done by the air that flowed over the *top* of the wing.

Air flowing across the rounded top of a wing goes faster because it has a longer way to go than the air flowing along the flat bottom. As a result, there is more pressure from below and the wing is forced upward. That is how a plane is held up as it travels along.

30

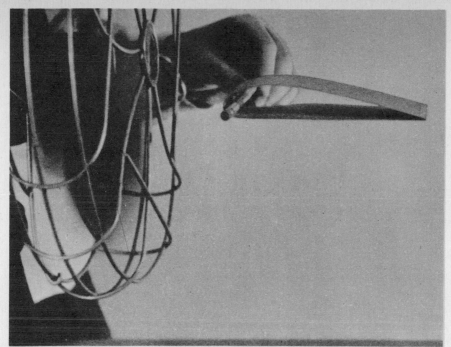

The wing flies . . .

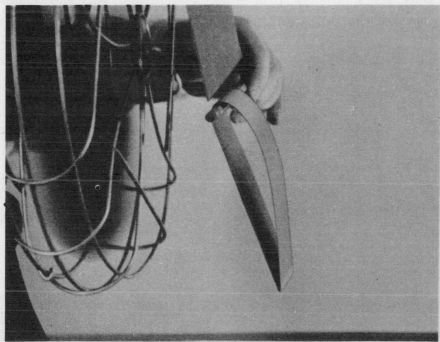

. . . until you cut off the air flow on top.

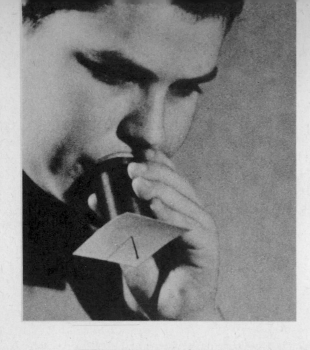

The harder
you blow, the
tighter it holds.

Try another experiment with moving air. Stick a pin halfway through a two-inch square of light cardboard. Hold the card flat against one end of a large spool with the pin inside the hole. The pin is there only to keep the card from sliding to one side.

Now blow hard and steadily through the spool, and you find that you no longer need to hold the card. It will not fall as long as there is a stream of air coming through the spool, even if you lean over so the spool faces downward.

The card stays in place for the same reason that the airplane wing was held up in the experiment on page 30. The still air below the card presses harder than the moving air above it, and so the card does not fall.

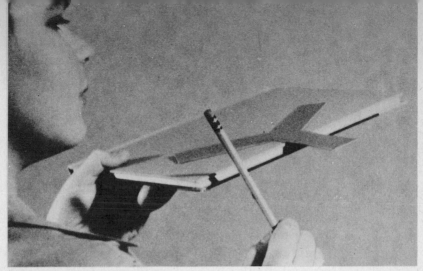

Cardboard boomerang.

A boomerang is an interesting weapon because it comes back to the thrower. The air makes the spinning boomerang tilt upward as it moves along. Then it begins to slip on the air and curves around to head back.

Make a boomerang by cutting a piece of stiff cardboard in this shape: The spaces between the three arms must be the same.

Lay the boomerang on a book with one of the arms over the edge, as in the picture. Tilt the book slightly upward and, with a sharp tap of a pencil, send the boomerang spinning away. It will swing around in a big circle and come back quite near to you.

It is easy to blow at a candle flame and make it bend away from you. But can you blow at a flame and make it bend *toward* you? It can be done if you know something about moving air.

For this experiment, set a lighted candle on a table. Blow at the flame gently. As you expect, it flutters and bends away from you. Then hold a dinner knife flat in front of the flame, about two inches away, as the picture shows. Blow again, and this time the flame bends *toward* you.

The air flowing around the edges of the knife breaks into little whirls. The whirling air curves around and swings back toward the blade, carrying the flame along.

Air flows smoothly around an object that has a streamlined shape. But it breaks up into whirls when it flows around an object that is not streamlined, such as the flat knife blade. The twisting streams of air drag along behind a moving object and hold it back. That is why airplanes and fast cars, trains, and boats must have streamlined shapes. It would take much greater power to move them along at high speed if they were flat at the front, or if they had uneven shapes.

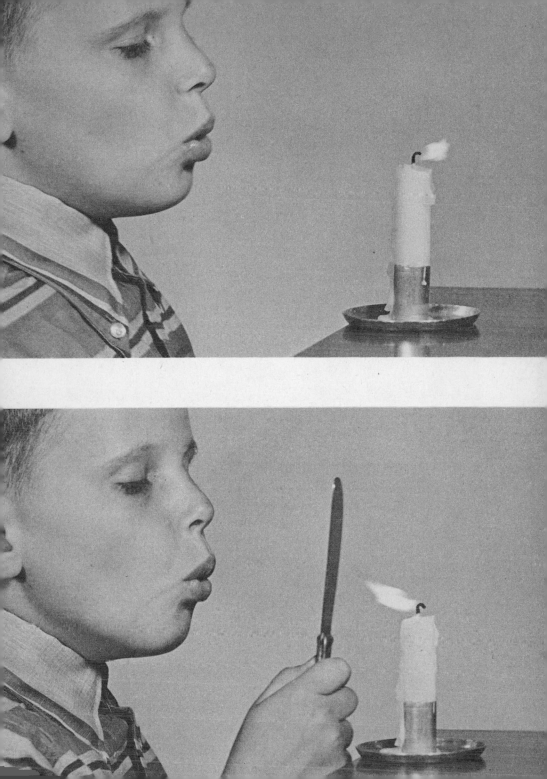

Everything that falls is slowed up by the air. A big object is held back more than a small one because it must push more air aside as it falls. The huge surface of a parachute gathers enough air to slow up the fall of the load it carries.

Make a parachute by tying the corners of a handkerchief to a spool with four pieces of string all the same length. Fold the parachute around the spool and throw it into the air. As it falls, the handkerchief will fill with air and float gently down. Without such a parachute to slow it down, the spool would dive to the ground.

SOUND AND MUSIC

If a stone is dropped into a quiet pond, waves spread out in circles over the water. Sound travels through the air in the same way, in the form of waves.

Sound waves are not exactly like the waves on water. The air in a sound wave has a push-and-pull motion, instead of moving up and down like the surface of water.

Any object that can shake back and forth very quickly sends out sound waves. This kind of back-and-forth movement is called **vibration.** When there are between 20 and 18,000 vibrations each second, your ear can hear a sound because your eardrums are set vibrating in step with the sound waves.

Every musical instrument has a part that can be made to vibrate. In a violin, the strings vibrate when they are rubbed with the bow. Blowing into a trumpet makes the air inside vibrate. The stretched head of a drum vibrates when it is hit with sticks. The faster a thing vibrates, the higher its tone will be.

Waves can do some surprising things. Two sets of waves coming from different places can pass right through each other without changing their shape.

Prove this by tossing two stones into a quiet pond or a large pan of water. One group of round ripples will cross directly through the other. Each will keep its shape, just as if the other were not there at all.

The same thing happens with sound waves. This explains why you can hear one person's words even though other people in the room are talking at the same time. The set of sound waves from each voice goes through the air without mixing up the others.

If you tap the side of an empty drinking glass with a pencil, the glass vibrates and gives off a tone. If some water is poured into the glass, the tone will be different, because the part of the glass that is free to vibrate is changed in size.

You can easily set up a homemade musical instrument. Fill seven drinking glasses with different amounts of water, to sound the notes of the scale. Keep adding the water slowly as you test each glass, until it gives off the proper note. Tap the glasses with a pencil to play simple songs.

Sound waves do this too.

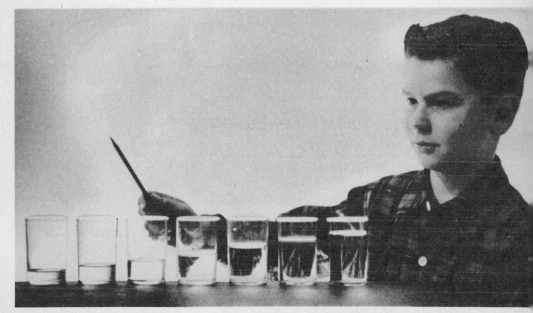

You can play tunes on the glasses.

When you strike a bell, the metal vibrates and starts up sound waves in the air. A bell is a curved piece of metal. A spoon is a curved piece of metal too, so it should be possible to get a bell-like tone by striking an ordinary spoon.

Get a tablespoon and a piece of string about five feet long. Tie the middle of the string tightly to the handle of the spoon. Hold one end of the string inside each ear with a finger, and let the spoon hang down freely, as in the picture.

Now swing the spoon gently, and let it strike against a table or chair. The sound you hear is surprisingly loud and clear, like the tone of a church bell.

The tone will seem loud only to you, and not to anyone standing near by. This is because most of the vibrations are carried directly to your ears through the string, instead of spreading through the air.

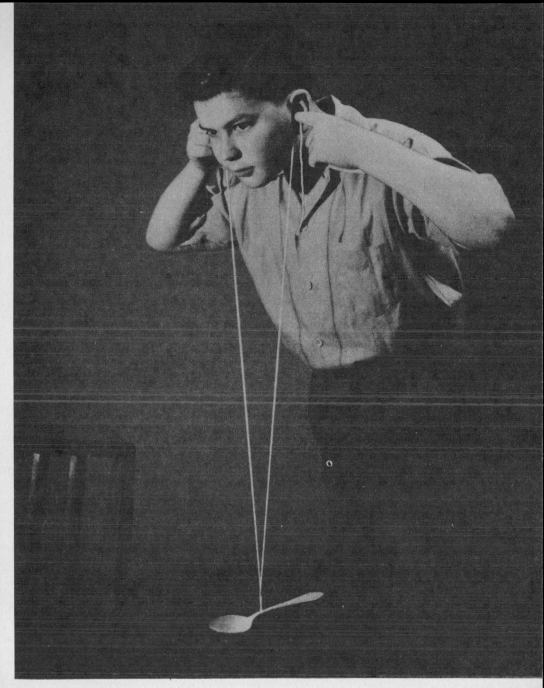

The sound is surprisingly loud.

Sound waves move through the air at a speed of about 1,100 feet a second. Light waves travel very much faster. You see a distant flash of lightning at once, but the sound of the thunder arrives later. Sound waves take about five seconds to go a mile.

You can figure out how far away a thunderstorm is. Count the number of seconds from the time you see a lightning flash until you hear the thunder. Divide this number by five, and the answer is the distance in miles. For instance, if the sound comes to you twenty seconds after you see the flash, you know that the storm is four miles away.

HOW HEAT ACTS

Heat can move from one place to another in different ways.

It can pass direct from a hot object to a cold one if the two touch each other. A spoon gets warm when it is put into a pan of hot water.

Heat may be carried by warmed air. A frying pan on the stove does not need to touch the flame. Air that is warmed by the flame rises to heat the pan.

You can also get heat from light — that is how you are warmed by the sun's rays. In the same way, you get heat from an open fire or an electric heater.

Adding or taking away heat can make great changes in materials. If you take enough heat away from water, it becomes solid. Then it is called ice. If you give enough heat to water, it becomes a gas that is called steam.

Giving heat to an object will make it expand, and cooling will make it shrink. Heat makes the mercury in an ordinary thermometer expand and push its way up the stem to mark a higher temperature.

If you put one end of a metal rod in a fire, the other end soon becomes too hot to hold. Heat passes along the rod very easily, because any metal is a good **conductor** of heat. Some materials do not conduct heat easily. That is why irons and frying pans have handles made of plastic or wood.

Touch a piece of metal and a piece of wood at the same time. The metal feels colder than the wood, even though both are at the same temperature. That is because the metal conducts heat away from your hand faster than the wood does.

About a hundred years ago, before there was electric lighting, there were often bad explosions in English coal mines. The miners used candles to light their way, and the open flames would sometimes set off gases that gathered in the mine. The great chemist, Sir Humphry Davy, thought of putting a wire cage around each candle. He figured that the metal wires would conduct the heat of the flame away before it could get through to the explosive gases. The idea worked, and the Davy Safety Lamp saved the lives of many miners.

See how metal wires conduct heat away. Lower a small piece of screen wire or an old wire strainer onto a candle flame. The flame is cut off, even though the screen is "full of holes."

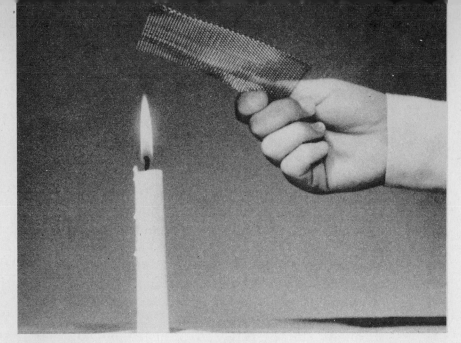

The metal screen is "full of holes"...

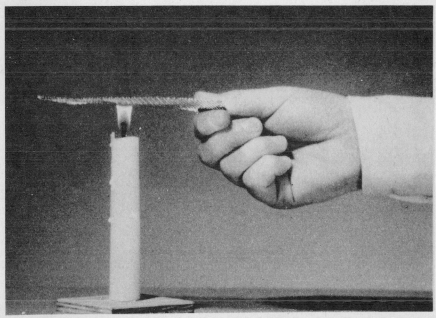

... but the flame does not get through.

Ice usually melts when the temperature gets up to 32 degrees. But you can melt ice just by squeezing it!

Fill a bread pan with water and place it in the freezer. When the water is frozen through, set the pan in warm water for a moment and then knock out the block of ice. Rest the ends on two wooden boxes, as the picture shows.

Hang a loop of thin, bare wire over the middle of the ice and tie a heavy rock to the ends of the loop. Place a pail underneath the hanging rock to catch the water that drips off the ice.

Soon you will notice that the wire is cutting into the ice. After a time it cuts completely throught, and the rock falls into the pail. But the block of ice remains whole and strong.

Pressure from the wire makes the ice melt where the wire touches it. The water from the melted ice flows around to the upper side of the wire and freezes again, leaving the block in one piece. The same thing happens when you "pack" a snowball. Pressure makes some of the snow melt. When you stop pressing, it freezes solid.

When you ice-skate, you really glide along on a thin layer of water, because the pressure of the blade melts some ice for a moment. In very cold weather, the pressure of the blade cannot melt the ice and skating is not good.

The block of ice remains whole after the wire has cut through.

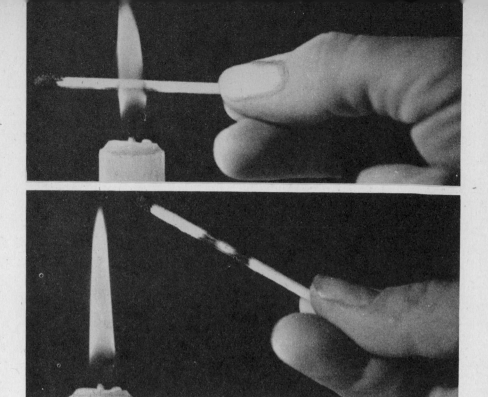

Interesting things happen when a candle burns. Heat from the flame makes the wax turn into a kind of mist that burns where it meets the air. This means that the flame is not as hot inside as at the edges, where the wax mist is burning.

Light a candle and keep the burned wooden matchstick. When the flame is steady, slide the matchstick sideways into it for a moment. The stick chars only in the two places where the outer layer of the flame touches it. The middle is not burned because it was in the cooler inner part of the flame.

ELECTRICITY

More than two thousand years ago, people found that small bits of wool would stick to a piece of amber that had been rubbed with a cloth. They did not know why this happened, but they described it as giving the amber a charge of **electricity**. "Electricity" is from the Greek word for amber.

If you scuff your shoes along a woolen rug, a charge of electricity builds up on your body. Then, by touching your finger to a radiator or faucet, you can feel a slight electric shock.

There are many other ways to build up a charge of electricity, but they work best in very dry weather. The least bit of moisture, even though you cannot see it, will let the charge leak away.

With the palm of your hand, rub a sheet of paper briskly and place it on the wall. The paper sticks to the wall, held there by the charge you produced. Next, pull the paper away. You will hear a crackling noise, which is really a little electrical storm. Benjamin Franklin did his famous kite experiment to show that lightning is nothing but a huge electric spark.

When a charge of electricity is allowed to move along a wire, it can do many useful things. It lights our buildings and runs motors, phones, radios, and TV sets.

Give a charge of electricity to a comb by running it through your hair several times. Slowly move the end of the charged comb toward a thin, steady stream of water. When the comb is about an inch away, the stream will start to bend toward it. This shows that things can be strongly attracted by nearby electric charges.

If you get the comb wet, the experiment may not work. And do not touch the faucet with the charged comb, because the electricity will leak off along the metal.

Sometimes friction in machinery will build up so much charge that it makes a spark and causes a fire or explosion. The way to prevent this is to help the charge leak away before too much gathers. The tires of a car rubbing on the road sometimes build up great amounts of charge. A special strap dragging from the axle leads the charge away to the ground.

A lightning rod on top of a house lets the huge charge on a cloud leak away to the ground without harming the building itself. The picture on page 42 shows a bolt of lightning striking a tall building. The steel frame safely carries the current to the earth.

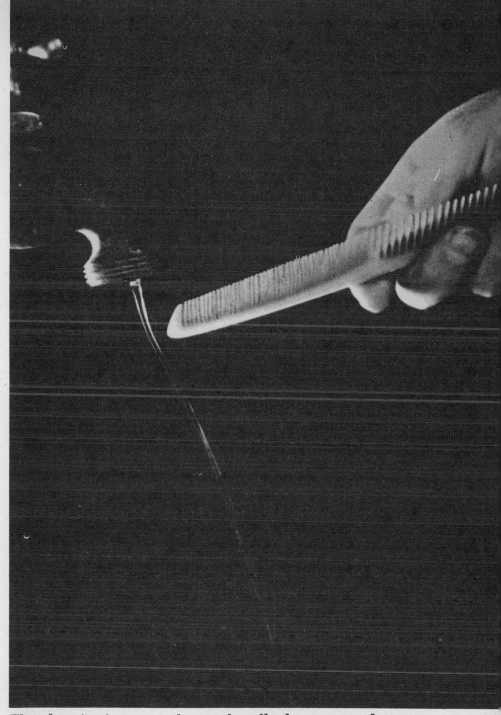

The electric charge on the comb pulls the stream of water.

Everything around you is made of **atoms** that are so tiny you would never guess they are there. For a long time, people thought an atom was the smallest possible bit of anything. Then scientists discovered that all atoms are made up of **protons, neutrons,** and **electrons** that are many thousands of times smaller than the atoms themselves.

Each kind of atom has a certain number of electrons. If you change the number of electrons, the atom gets an electric charge. Do an experiment in which you add some electrons to atoms and then take them away.

Crumple a piece of tissue paper to form a ball the size of a marble. Cover the ball completely with a piece of aluminum foil. Hang the ball by a long thread.

Give a comb an electric charge by running it through your hair several times. As you do this, electrons from the atoms of your hair stick to atoms of the comb.

Touch the hanging ball lightly several times with the comb, to let some of the electrons go over to the ball. Now the ball will back away from the comb, as the first picture shows. This is because the extra electrons on the ball and the electrons on the comb push each other apart.

You can get rid of the extra electrons on the ball. Hold a lighted candle under it for a moment, and the ball falls back against the comb. In the candle flame there are atoms that have lost some electrons. As these atoms rise, they take the extra electrons away from the ball and it loses its charge.

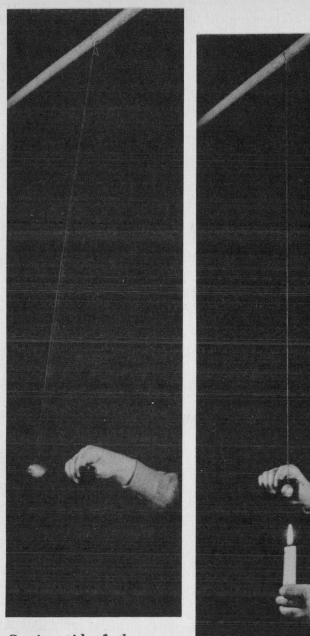

Getting rid of electrons.

When electricity flows through a wire, it produces magnetism. The current in the wire coils of an electric motor builds up a strong magnetic force than can do useful work. Such motors run refrigerators, elevators, trains, and many other kinds of machines.

Make a lifting magnet. Take about ten feet of bell wire and wind it on a big nail. Put one turn right next to another, always going around the nail in the same direction. Make several layers, and keep the turns in place by fastening the end ones with tape. Leave about a foot of wire at each end.

Tape together two flashlight cells so that the bottom of one makes good contact with the top of the other. Scrape the covering off the ends of the wire and tape one end firmly to the bottom of the lower cell. Put a small pile of carpet tacks on the table, and you are ready to test your magnet.

Press the loose end of the wire to the top post of the cell. At the same time, lower the point of the nail into the pile of tacks. Slowly raise the nail and most of the tacks come with it. Now lift the wire away from the battery. This stops the current and the tacks drop off the nail.

The nail is a magnet only while there is an electric current in the coil. This kind of magnet is called an **electromagnet**.

The nail is a magnet . . .

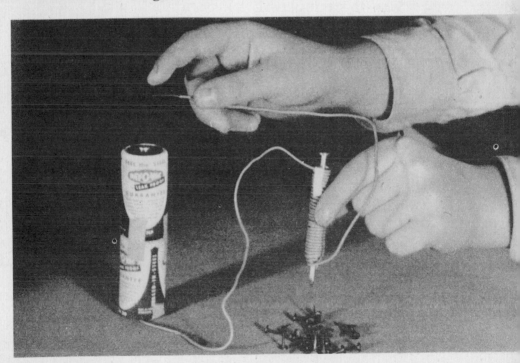

. . . only while the current is on.

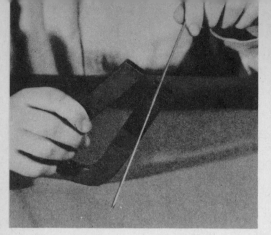
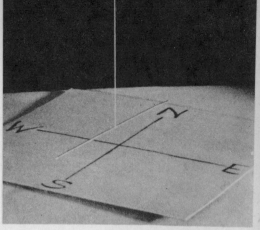

Long ago, people discovered that certain kinds of rocks were natural magnets. If they hung one of these rocks so that it could turn easily, it always swung around to a north-and-south position. They did not know why this happened, but they made good use of the magnetic rocks as compasses. Later, scientists discovered that the earth itself is a huge magnet that pulls the compass into a north-and-south position.

These days, magnets are usually made by electricity, as in the experiment with the electromagnet. But if you already have a magnet, you can make others from it without using electricity. Try this by making a compass.

Get a toy magnet and a steel knitting or darning needle. Rub the needle along one end of the magnet with smooth strokes about twenty times, always rubbing in the same direction. Then hang the needle by a thread over a card marked North, South, East, and West, and you have a compass.

LIGHT AND SEEING

Anything that glows sends out waves of light. Light waves come from the sun, a firefly, a candle flame or a light bulb.

Very few objects that we see send out their own light waves. Most things are seen by **reflected** waves. The sun shines on a house, and the waves bounce off to your eyes. At night, if the lamps in a room are turned off, there are no light waves to be reflected and you cannot see anything in the room.

When light strikes an object, some of the waves are reflected, and some go right through if the material is clear, like water or glass.

Sunlight is a mixture of light of every color. You can see these colors when they are spread out in a rainbow.

In outer space, light travels about 186,000 miles a second. It goes a little slower in air, water, and glass, but still nearly a million times as fast as a jet plane.

AMERICAN STOCK PHOTO, FROM FREDERIC LEWIS

An important and interesting fact about light is that it travels in straight lines. Except under very special conditions, light does not bend around things that are in its path.

A carpenter sights along a board to see if it is flat. If light waves did not move in straight lines, this could not be done.

The beam from a searchlight is perfectly straight. The searchlight can be swung around and pointed in any direction, but the beam of light will always go through the air in a straight line.

Make some shadow pictures to show how light travels. Use direct sunlight or the light from a slide projector. The boy in the lower picture is holding his hands in a way that makes the shadow on the wall look like a dog's head. Notice also that the boy and his shadow match exactly.

You can make shadow pictures only because the light goes in straight lines past the edge of the thing that is making the shadow.

Light waves travel in straight lines when they are in material that is the same all the way through. But as soon as they pass into a different material, they bend aside and go off in a new direction. This change in direction is called **refraction**. For example, light is refracted when it goes from water into air.

Hold a pencil in a bowl of water, as in the picture. Look at the pencil from above and a little to one side. The lower part of the pencil seems to be bent sharply upward.

That is what happens: You can see the pencil because it reflects light to your eyes. But light waves reflected to your eyes from the underwater part of the pencil must go through two materials. As the light leaves the water and goes into the air, it is refracted in such a way that the pencil seems to be bent sharply upward.

There are other ways in which you can see this kind of refraction. An object behind a strip of glass may look broken into several pieces as the light waves go from air to glass and back to air again. If you look down into a clear, quiet pool of water, the bottom seems to slope upward in front of you because of refraction.

Refraction of light makes the pencil look bent.

A **lens** is a piece of glass or other clear material that has smoothly curved sides. Lenses are useful for bending light waves in special ways.

Water sometimes acts as a lens. Look at a table-cloth through a glass of water, and notice how the weave of the cloth is magnified. A modern microscope uses sets of several lenses and can make tiny objects look hundreds of times bigger than they really are.

Things usually seem to be turned around when you look at them directly through the lens. The reason is that the light waves coming from each side of an object cross inside the lens and come out on the opposite side. You can see this happen by doing an experiment.

Get a card and a glass of water. Draw an arrow on the card and stand it up on a table. Set the glass of water down a little to one side of the card, a few inches in front of it.

Stand about three feet from the card and stoop down until your eyes are on a level with the arrow. Notice which way the arrow points, and then slide the glass until it is between the card and your eyes. The arrow that you see through the water now points the opposite way. This shows that the light waves from each end of the arrow crossed when they passed through the water lens.

Slide the glass of water in and out a few times and watch the arrow turn around.

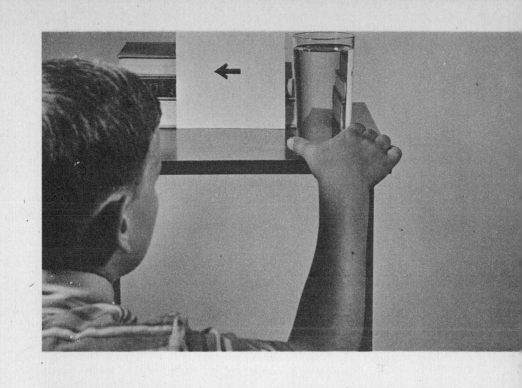

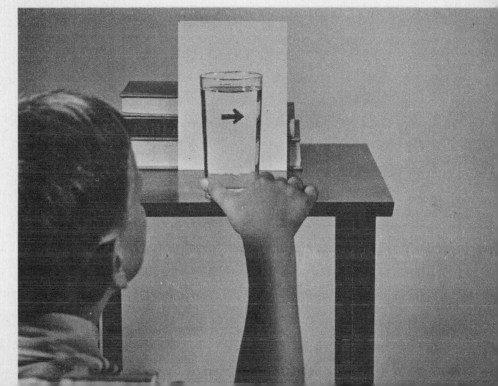

Your eyes are wonderful little cameras that give you a motion picture in color of the things around you. The eye has a lens that gathers light on the sensitive back surface, called the **retina**. Nerves from the retina give the brain a report of what you see.

There is one spot in your eye which is blind! This is the place where the nerve bundle is joined to the retina. If any light happens to fall at this point, you do not see it.

> To find the *blind spot*, hold this page a little more than a foot from your face. Keep your left eye closed, and look at the cross with your right eye. You also see the dot and the triangle.
>
> Now keep looking at the cross with your right eye as you slowly bring the book closer. You will find a place when the triangle disappears as your view of it falls on the blind spot. Slowly move the book still closer, and the dot becomes invisible — but the triangle appears again.